Lamoussa Théodore KAFANDO

LA FEMME DE MON PÈRE N'EST PAS MA MÈRE

(Théâtre)

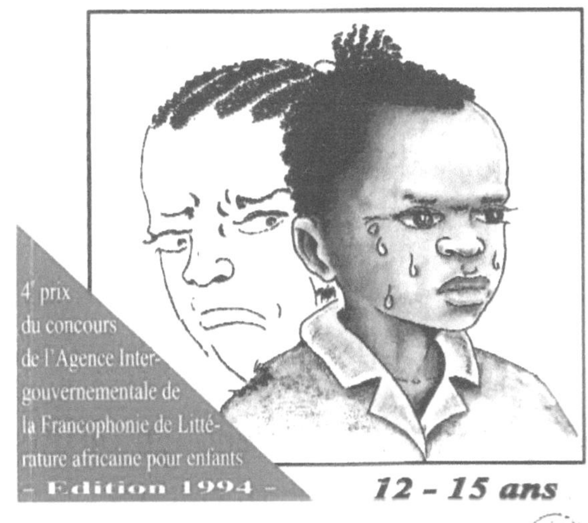

My Father's wife is not my Mother

A Play by

Award Winning Playwright Lamoussa Theodore Kafando

1

OVERVIEW

(On stage, children are playing hopscotch. Suddenly, one of the players, the group leader, stops everything!)

THE GROUP LEADER

I am tired! I have had of enough of this. Let's play another game.

THE FIRST PLAYER

Me too! I have had of enough of this. I say, let's play a game of riddles!

The First Riddle: In a particular village, everybody is dead. So, everybody is tied together with one piece of rope. What do you call that?

Response: Actually, it is a broom, or a bundle of wood attached to the string!

The Second Riddle: One day, I bought a sheep for my farm. When I started slaughtering it, I did not see any blood; but, when I started eating eat, I saw some blood. What was I really eating?

Response: It was a red kola nut that I broke in half and ate! (The kola nut is a favorite snack that is red on the outside and yellowish on the inside.)

THE SECOND PLAYER

Now, I have had enough of all of these riddles. Everybody sit down! I am going to tell you a little story… a fantastic story! Now, everybody listen carefully. One day the long-eared rabbit was hopping around in the field.

THE GROUP LEADER

Ok, thanks my friend. You don't need to continue this story. Everybody knows it already. Let's do something else. My friends, do you all like theatrical plays?

THE OTHER CHILDREN

Yes! Yes! We love to see plays!

THE GROUP LEADER

Then, I am going to ask all of you to go backstage to get ready and then come back and act out this play entitled: ***My Father's wife is not my Mother!***

THE FIRST PLAYER

My father's wife is not my mother, hmmm! That sounds like it's going to be an interesting story! Is this an action or comedy that will make us all laugh?

THE GROUP LEADER

A comedy or not, I promise you all that you will be delighted after you see this play ***My father's wife is not my mother!*** Quick, let's go backstage, my friends.

(The actors go backstage while a little soft music is playing in the background)

ACT I
Scene I

(Today is Thursday, a day off for the students. Clemence and Zozou, both CM1*students, are at home. Clemence is eating some cookies. Zouzou is studying.

***CMI – 6th Grade**

CLEMENCE

Zouzou! Look at these golden cookies glazed with honey! They are some incredibly good cookies, round and flat! But you're not getting any!

ZOUZOU

Listen Clemence! Don't tease me. I didn't ask you what you were eating.

CLEMENCE

Oh really? I know you want some of my cookies. Tell the truth, is it true that you don't like cookies glazed with honey? You know they're better than that plate of millet with kapok vegetables that gets all over your lips?

ZOUZOU

Clemence! Clemence! Get away from me, you are preventing me from studying for my classes.

CLEMENCE

Your studies! Your studies! Can anybody really study when they are hungry? Don't be ashamed to ask me: "Give me some of those golden, honey glazed cookies!" Stop beating around the bush, like our teacher always says! A hungry beggar should be ashamed to ask for something to eat!

ZOUZOU

(Angry)

You'd better watch it Clemence! Don't insult me like that! Am I a beggar? Get out of here, if not, I am going to beat you like a dog who stole a piece of meat from the butcher.

CLEMENCE

Beat me like a dog! Who do you think I am? Why don't you just say that we are simply going to fight it out?

ZOUZOU

You know, Clemence, between you and me, there is no match! Your size and your height are only fooling you!

CLEMENCE

Are you jealous of my overweight? Well, I am proud of it. I eat well because my mother feeds me well. Can your poor mother do the same thing?

ZOUZOU

(Like a flash of lightening, he jumps on Clemence and slaps her. The fight starts. The cookies hit the floor and Clemence touches Zouzou's notebook with her greasy hands. Clemence is thrown to the floor during the heated clash.)

You ugly thing! You'll think twice before insulting my mother again!

CLEMENCE

(On the ground, shouting and insulting Zouzou)

You idiot, you took me by surprise. If you hurt me, you'll see what's going to happen! You will never get chance to beat me up, you little brat! My mother will take care of you too! Let me get myself up from here and we'll continue this fight and we're going to really see what happens when I put your face in the dirt.

(She shouts…and the outburst alerts Zouzou's mother who comes over to separate the two fighters and she sends them away from one another.

Scene II

Clemence's mother, returning from the market, finds her daughter in tears, and her dress is dirty and torn.

CHARLOTTE
(Surprised)

Clemence! What happened to you? Who beat you up like that to the point of dirtying and tearing up your dress?

CLEMENCE
(Wiping her tears away)

It was little Zouzou who started a fight with me. Every time that you are not here, he calls me a bum and a bad little girl. Then, today he called me names and to pay him back, I called him a puny little boy, skinny and not well-raised.

Afterwards, he got angry, and he hit me first. We fought and he was jealous about my pretty dress, he started tearing it up. Then, his mother came to break up the fight.

CHARLOTTE

Oh no! Things like that shouldn't happen. It is about time that little square head ZouZou learns how to control himself! I am going to teach him a lesson by no longer tolerating his foolishness.

Alimata! Alimata! Come here with your little Zouzou.
(Alimata and Zouzou arrive)

CHARLOTTE

Alimata, tell me what happened before Zouzou and Clemence started fighting like chickens in a cock fight. Also, why did you decide to hold my daughter while your little rascal Zouzou was fighting her? Did you see what he did to my daughter's dress? That is a pretty dress that her uncle just gave her from his recent trip to Europe.

ALIMATA

Charlotte don't get upset. Your daughter certainly has lied to you. I could never do anything that like that as you are thinking. Clemence and Zouzou are both my children, in my eyesight.

CHARLOTTE

So, are you trying to call me a liar? Well, at any rate, I'd rather be a liar than a witch!

ALIMATA

Charlotte, who are you calling a witch?

CHARLOTTE

The guilty one who has the loudest mouth.

ALIMATA

I don't feel like the guilty one but beware of the no-good lady who treats me as though I am a witch.

CHARLOTTE

No good lady or not, you are not far from being a witch since your little bad boy Zouzou and you tried to kill my daughter Clemence, while I was not around.

ALIMATA

(she couldn't keep her cool)

Me, a witch? Well, it was your mother who taught me how to do evil things. So, watch your mouth Charlotte. Let's stop this discussion about little children's disputes.

CHARLOTTE

Alimata, you're insulting my mother like that? Now, you are adding fuel to the fire, just to get everybody upset. Alimata, what can you do to me? You are simply a witch full of watery eyes. Do you believe that I am fooled by all your little tricks of trying to break-up me and Oumarou? It is you Alimata, who is going to be the one to leave this house.

ALIMATA

Enough of this, you foolish busybody! If you weren't pregnant, I would prove to you that I am a true woman!

CHARLOTTE

Hey! Hey! Alimata, despite my being nearly full-term pregnant, what can you even do to me? Besides, it is this pregnancy that is making you so aggressive and jealous. (She begins to take off her clothe).

ALIMATA

Charlotte, it is simply useless for you to start removing your clothe. I respect the fact that you are pregnant, if not, you would see that an iron pipe and a bamboo stick do not cross one another in a field of battle. (She grabs ZouZou by the arm and she goes back to her room).

CHARLOTTE

You'd better go back to your room; if not, I will make you see a million starts in the daylight! At any rate, I am going to tell Oumarou everything that happened.

(She also takes her daughter by the arm and goes towards her room, while mumbling).

Scene III

(Oumarou comes back from work)

OUMAROU

(Moaning while laying on a mat).

OUMAROU

Charlotte, what's wrong with you? Is everything all right? I hope these are not signs of early childbirth, right?

CHARLOTTE

Who knows? It could be the sign of a miscarriage since I never have any peace in this house because of your wife Alimata.

OUMAROU

Don't tell me that you two were fighting again and that you beat one another like children!

CHARLOTTE

Oumarou, yeah! That's right! It was a trivial story between children that spiraled into a dispute between adults. During, our neck-to-neck battle, she hit me very hard in my stomach. You are really lucky to find me alive. My daughter Clemence, she too was almost beaten to death. Look at what happened to dress that all the children in the neighborhood likes. (while moaning again) God, help me!

OUMAROU

Charlotte, where was Zouzou's grandfather when you all were arguing?

CHARLOTTE

As usual, he was at some little old restaurant. He came back just when we finished fighting.

OUMAROU

Well, I am going to take you to the maternity hospital because you never know! If everything is all right, when I get back, I am going to straighten out all this jealousy between the two of you.

CHARLOTTE

Thank you Oumarou. I took some sedatives. Perhaps from now on, things will get better. The pain is not that bad. I only ask you to allow me to go to my mother's house to give birth, because my life is in danger here.

OUMAROU

Oh, your life will not be in danger. I am the one in charge here. The one who does not behave, will get out immediately, without a second thought.

Alimata! Alimata! Come here with Zouzou.

ALIMATA

Here I am!

OUMAROU

Oh, you're here. Well thanks a lot! Without saying anything you are going back to your parents' home. Just get all your things and go back to your parents' house.

ALIMATA

What did I do that was so serious that I deserve to be thrown out of the house?

OUMAROU

Oh, you don't know what you did? You'll know once you're staying with your parents. I can no longer stand your foolishness. There has always been issues of jealousy, to no end, ever since I married Charlotte as my second wife. Just look at yourself! Look at Clemence's dress. You must have been a witch from birth to ack like you did…hitting a pregnant woman in the stomach, isn't that a crime?

ALIMATA

You believe that gossip from Charlotte?

OUMAROU

It's no longer about believing or not believing. I know the facts. So, Alimata, don't get on my last nerves.

ALIMATA

Well, since you don't want to listen to me and you are agreeing with Charlotte's lies, I don't have a choice. I am going to leave if that's what you want.

OUMAROU

It is not what I want, it is an order. Just pack up your bags, I don't want to see you in this house anymore.

(*He gets ready to hit Alimata when grandfather stops him beforehand.*)

OUMAROU

Hey Oumarou, what is going on here?

OUMAROU

Dad, I am just tired of Alimata's foolishness. She does not want to get along with her a co-spouse. I think somebody must be a murderer when they dare hit a pregnant woman, who is almost ready to deliver, in the stomach.

GRANDFATHER

My son, are you sure that Alimata really hit Charlotte?

OUMAROU

Sure! If that were not the case, do you think that Charlotte would make-up a story from her imagination?

OUMAROU

My son, I cannot say yes or no. I can only recommend that you try to understand the reason for their misunderstanding. When two co-spouses quarrel, avoid taking sides with one or the other. Be careful!

OUMAROU

Since I married Charlotte, she doesn't want to have anything to do with her. Father, look at Charlotte's and my daughter'. Patience has its limits. Charlotte must leave my house now!

ZOUZOU
(touched by her father's behavior)

Daddy, what did Mommy do? Are you kicking her out of the house?

OUMAROU

Your mother is nothing but a witch. She knows what she did. She just must leave this house!

ZOUZOU
(*crying*)

Daddy, can I go with Mommy?

OUMAROU

No, go get your books and start studying your subjects.

(*The neighbors, overhearing the child's mother crying, arrive and run, in vain, to help cool Oumarou down. Music plays behind the stage*)

ACT II

NARRATION:

Dear spectators, as you just witnessed, Charlotte has succeeded in chasing her co-spouse, Alimata, away. Now, she

Hopes to live in harmony with her husband Oumarou. But, as time passes by, she realizes that there is always an obstacle that prevents the couple from moving forward. So, the story doesn't end there! Listen and watch!

Scene I

(As on every Thursday, Zouzou is at home)

CHARLOTTE

Zouzou! Zouzou!

ZOUZOU

Yes, Mommy Charlotte!

CHARLOTTE

Have you finish sweeping the rooms, washing the dishes, cleaning the pots, tiding up the kitchen and filling up the water barrel?

ZOUZOU

Yes, mommy, I finished all of the house chores.

CHARLOTTE

Ok, now you can have some free time, but don't go too far because I might send you to the butcher to buy some meat for the meal tomorrow.

ZOUZOU

I understand mommy. I won't go far away. I will sit next to the container of water to study my lessons.

GRANDFATHER

(Smoking his pipe, gets up and walks toward Zouzou)

Zouzou, what are you doing now?

ZOUZOU

Grandfather, I am studying my history lesson. Tomorrow is Friday and we will be studying history.

GRANDFATHER

I wanted you to go with me to visit your Aunt Sabine. It has been a long time since I paid her a visit.

ZOUZOU

Ok, I'm coming Grandfather, I'm coming. I am going to ask Mommy Charlotte and then we'll go!

He runs to Charlotte who is knitting). Mommy Charlotte, Grandfather asked me to go with him to Aunt Sabine's house.

CHARLOTTE

(She dares not to even move her head.)

You're not leaving this place! I told you not to go far from here.

ZOUZOU

But Mommy Charlotte, Grandfather is the one who asked me to go with him.

CHARLOTTE

Do I have to tell you again? You are not moving one inch from this place.

ZOUZOU

Mommy Charlotte, we are not going to be long.

CHARLOTTE (Angrily)

You imbecile! I told you that you are not leaving here. Your grandfather can go by himself! He surely knows the way. He's not blind.

GRANDFATHER

(Surprised, he walks a couple of steps towards Charlotte)

You're exaggerating, my daughter-in-law: you are refusing to allow my little

Zouzou to go with me to "Sabine's house? You know very well that it is a pleasure for an old man to go in the company of his grandchild.

CHARLOTTE

Well, I am not against that; but today Zouzou is not going with you. I categorically refuse to allow Zouzou to go with you and you cannot make me change my mind.

GRANDFATHER

Charlotte, I really don't understand you!

CHARLOTTE

You don't understand me? Do I have to make myself be understood? I have had enough of your disgusting remarks concerning me.

GRANDFATHER
(Shaking his head)

Charlotte, since Alimata's departure, I guess that you don't even want me here in this house. Well, did you forget that it was my wife and I who begged my son Oumarou to accept you as his wife? Today, I have become your enemy to fight with! Well, we'll see about that!

CHARLOTTE

Hey! Hey "Ok we'll see!" Don't you dare beat me up! Since more than seven years, you have never dreamt of going back to where you came from. All you do is look me up and down with your evil eyes. Nothing I do escapes you. You could do better looking somewhere else. Ugh!

GRANDFATHER

Well thanks Charlotte. I guess that I measure up to your words and gestures. I want you to know that if I am worthy of my father, my ancestors, the gods of the rivers and mountains who saw when I was born, it won't happen like you want it with your burning desires! We'll see!

CHARLOTTE

Hey! Hey! Hey! Your threats hardly scare me!

(She pouts, as a sign of disdain, then she starts turning on the tape recorder to listen to some music. Grandfather, furious, leaves and passes by Therese, Charlotte's friend, as she enters…)

THERESE

Hello Charlotte. Oh, you're listening to some good music while knitting?

CHARLOTTE

Hello my dear friend. Music can calm down anger sometimes. This old music reminds me of some good memories.

THERESE

That's true! But what are you knitting? Do you have some orders to fill?

CHARLOTTE

No! I am just knitting some baby clothes for my future baby.

THERESE

Another pregnancy? Wow! Childbirths one after another don't make you tired?

CHARLOTTE

Yes. But, does one have any other choice one is born a woman? You just have to give birth, bring children into the world.

THERESE

Yes, bring children into the world, but you have to take care of them very well. The time between childbirth, these days, must be taken in consideration in the household for two fundamental reasons:

- Childbirths that are too close together can tire the mother out and put a strain on her health.

-   Couples who bring children into the world like ants always have a problem raising and educating them.

CHARLOTTE

You are right my friend, but my husband detests all these new contraceptive methods.

(She remembers that she did not ask her friend to have a seat)

Excuse-me. Therese, sit down.

THERESE

Thanks, Charlotte. went to the hairdressers.

(Therese takes a few steps to show off her clothes)

CHARLOTTE

Ah! What a pretty dress you have! You never told me that you had such a pretty one like that! Who gave you that gift?

THERESE

It is my husband who gave this to me from his recent trip to France.

CHARLOTTE

Eh! You, that old husband of yours! He only thinks about you and he only lives for you.

THERESE

But Charlotte, tell me, where is Alimata, your co-spouse.

CHARLOTTE

Oumarou finally decided to get rid of that wild woman; but I will still never have any peace in this house. When you were on your way here, you didn't run into my brother-in-law?

THERESE

Sure, I ran into some old man who responded to my greeting in a casual way.

CHARLOTTE

Oh yeah? That old guy is really against me. He thinks it is I who is managing his son's salary to the detriment of his parents.

Today, more than ever, his actions and words prove that he doesn't like me.

Oh, poor me!

THERESE

My dear friend, you know that when a brother-in-law or a sister-in-law gets in the middle of a couple, it is simply poison! But I think that Oumarou's father is rather reasonable.

CHARLOTTE

Reasonable? That's what you say! My father-in-law has become my undisputed co-spouse. Nothing that I do escapes him. But tell me, my friend, what would you do if you were in my shoes?

THERESE

If I were in your shoes, hmmm… he would have left a long time ago.

CHARLOTTE

Oh well! What you said just gave me an idea. This evening, if he doesn't leave, I will ask him for a divorce.

THERESE

Oh, you are reacting too quickly. I am running along to my beauty salon.

CHARLOTTE

Already? Chatting is remarkably interesting and now you are in a hurry to leave?

THERESE

I don't want to miss my appointment. I am going to the beauty shop "so I can look better", you got to keep your appointments!

(Charlotte accompanies Therese to the door and she comes back to get ready to confront her husband).

Scene II

(Oumarou comes home drunk, and he finds his wife Charlotte looking sad.)

OUAROU

My dear! How are you doing? Why are you looking so sad? But, honey, tell me… what is wrong?

CHARLOTTE

I want you to understand that I no longer want to live with you.

OUAROU

And why is that? Tell me dear, what is really the matter?

CHARLOTTE

Oumarou, I am telling you that I can no longer live with you. Your father has become like my undisputed co-spouse. Nothing that I do escapes him. He is profiting from Alimata's departure so he can threaten me to death. With his insults and his threats, I think, Oumarou, that I can no longer live with you, it is either him or me, your wife!

OUMAROU

Oh, stop crying, Charlotte! I am going to put this house in order. (He calls Zouzou) Zouzou! Zouzou! Come here! (The child comes forth) Is your grandfather here?

ZOUZOU

Yes, he's lying on his lounge chair.

OUMAROU

Well, I'm going to see him. (He joins the old man), Dad, I came to see you.

GRAND-FATHER

That's good, my son. What do you want from me?

OUMAROU

Father, I came to inform you about some serious problems that never cease to occur in my house. And these serious problems are caused by you. So, you should be the only one to go counsel us on the best way to live in harmony in the family. Instead of staying in the village with your friends who are producing tons and tons of peanuts, in the field, you want to stay here to sow all this discord in my house. I have had enough of all of these disputes with my wife.

GRAND-FATHER

Listen my son, I don't know what has happened to you. If you have had a lot of alcohol then, go and rest then when you are sober, you can come back and see me.

OUMAROU

Who was drinking? Are you treating me like a drunkard? You threaten my wife every day and you don't even want me to talk about it?

GRAND-FATHER

Is that what Charlotte told you? I think that you should be more responsible before spilling out the milk on someone. You don't even know that it is your wife who always provokes me, wishing that I would die? (Shaking his head) it is true that each day becomes more glamorous or dreary along with the passing of time. My son, when I went to ask her parent's approval for your marriage, I surely didn't know that one day she would hate me. Today, for Charlotte, I am simply an enemy to fight with. My son, it is not serious, I am going to pack my bag.

(He starts taking steps to leave the house. Oumarou continues to run his mouth.)

OUMAROU

Hey, we'd better finish with this foolishness. The old man is going back to the village right away today.

GRAND-FATHER

(He comes back with little suitcase under his arm)

Yes, the old man is happy to return to the village. My son, I am going away, my soul is at peace, knowing that I have Zouzou, my grandson who will be able to tell me, one day, the rest of all these events if God would give me more years to live. I'll see you later or good-bye, my little ZouZou. God will help me to renew the roof of my farmhouse in the village despite my old age strength. Good-bye… (*he leaves*).

CHARLOTTE

(Listening while hiding away and she shouts for joy)

Ha! Ha! Ha! The old man has finally decided to leave. Now, I will have some peace in this house.

OUMAROU

(Looks at his father walking away, and he is surprised by his wife's behavior)

Charlotte, this makes you laugh? You think that it makes me happy to chase my father way from the house?
(Silence)

If I did that, it was simply to avoid a lot of arguments.

(A moment afterwards, here comes the old man again. Oumarou hurries to ask him ...)

What is the matter now? What are you looking for?

GRAND-FATHER

Don't worry, my son. If I came back, it is only to humbly ask you to find me a blanket that could protect me from the cold in the village.

OUMAROU

Zouzou! Zouzou! Come go to my room, look on the bed, and you will find a blanket. Bring it here.

ZOUZOU
(speaking in a low voice)

Problems, problems all over the house!

(Oumarou gets angry because Zouzou
is taking too much time to leave the
room

OUMAROU

Zouzou! Zouzou! What are you doing in
the room?

*(Zouzou comes out, with scissors in his
hands and half of the blanket).*

OUMAROU

But Zouzou, what did you do? What are
you holding? Are you crazy?
(He gets ready to hit Zouzou).

ZOUZOU

Oh! Papa, you are angry to see me cut
the blanket into two equal parts? That is
so simple. And guess what? If I cut this

beautiful blanket into to equal parts, it is for you to give half of it to my grandfather. I saved the other half for as long as I could and once I grow up like you, I will chase you away from the house and give it to you. (He starts crying.)

OUMAROU
(Hit like a strike of lightning speaking in a monologue)

What did I do? Where am I? Who am I? What am I doing? Oh! What type of life is this? Who gave me advice to marry two wives? I can't even sleep. I no longer have any peace. Problems and more problems, it seems like they never end. The wives get jealous of one another. The children want to fight each other. The one to whom I had confidence in does not even what to be around my own father. To search for a way to balance out everything, I drown my problems in alcohol. Poor me! While I am alive, the children of my two wives act like dogs and cats, what will happen after I die? Poor me…polygamy! Now, I understand it. (He gets himself together and he calls Charlotte).

Charlotte, Charlotte! No son in Africa should chase his own father from his house. But, if you find it impossible to live with me and my father, I find myself with the difficult decision to chase my father from the house. You can pack all of your things; the door is wide open.

CHARLOTTE
(Crying)

Oumarou, where do you want me to go? Who will accept me as a wife? Oumarou, look at my situation! I am eight and half months pregnant.

Oumarou, ask the old man not to leave. Ask him, in the name of his ancestors, to stay here. From now on, this is the end of our arguments.

OUMAROU

Father, I ask you for forgiveness. It is the effects of alcohol that caused me to act like a fool. Both my wife and I ask you to forgive us.

GRANDFATHER

I forgive you. But, if truly I seem to be an obstacle to the harmony of your family, with grace, please accept that I return to the village.

GRANDFATHER

Oumarou, I am proud of you now. You have become a true father of the family, a true responsible man.

Together, let's burst into joy!

(Music)

Scene III

(The Return of Alimata. Reconciliation)

Father, we burst into joy. Alimata, little Zouzou's mother is here, with us. The abusive words between the co-spouses are buried as of today and are exchanged for the happiness of the family.

Father, I knew that acting out of character, I would cause our children to suffer.

GRAND-FATHER

My son, life is an inexhaustible source of wisdom. It is the carrier of happiness and sadness, of glory and of dishonor.

The children inherit from their parents. I know that polygamy has not always been a good thing, but once it is consummated, you must work to create understanding, harmony in the midst of the family, for raising the children.

Dear daughters-in-law, from now on, I am counting on your understanding in order to ban all the dangerous quarrels for the benefit of love between all of our great family members united in solidarity.

ALIMATA

Father, I am infinitely grateful unto you. I loved your son. We got married for better and for worse. He married a second wife, Charlotte, whom I had always considered as "my little sister". But unfortunately I remember that Charlotte did not want to support me in the house. The proof: it is with her pressure that Oumarou made me pack my bags and go back to live with my parents. If today peace is restored, then it is because of you and Almighty God!

CHARLOTTE

I am ashamed of myself for having acted like that. However, Alimata and I, live like little chicks in the same nest so that Oumarou, our husband can assure our happiness.

As for the children, I think that they will follow our advice that will be full of wisdom and they will take into consideration their future life, all the tenderness of all of our works and deeds, solidarity, understanding and love, *(while turning towards the children)* Clemence! Zouzou! It that understood?

CLEMENCE AND ZOUZOU

Yes, mama. From now on, we will get along just fine!

OUMAROU

My dear children, I am relieved. All of you come, we are going to celebrate this unforgettable day over a good meal!

(Family meal. Family atmosphere of celebration with a musical selection)

My Father's Wife is not My Mother

The author, Lamoussa Theodore Kafando, was born in 1943 in Zitenga, Burkina Faso, West Africa. He is both an instructor and a cultural animator specialist. Currently, he is the Director the National Prix of Ouagadougou. Several times, Lamoussa Theodore Kafando was the winner of the national competition of storytelling, theater, poetry, and children's drawing competition.

-In 1993, his work entitled **Laafi Nooma or Health"** won the 2nd Prize of the Intergovernmental Agency of Francophone African Literature for Children.

-In 1994, Intergovernmental Agency of Francophone African Literature for Children awarded him 3rd Prize for his play *My Father's Wife is not My Mother*."

-In 1995, he received the 1st Place Award of The Francophone African Literature for Children for his short story, *The Handicapped Girl from Taab-Gninga.*

This book: In this short play, (2 acts, 6 scenes), while presenting words and acts in a serious tragedy-comedy, Kafando seriously undertakes the task of correcting of the stubborn blemishes that exist in African societies: polygamy.

In this play, the wisdom of the old man would have been right concerning the unjust brutality of polygamous husbands such as slanderous jealousy between two wives and the ongoing intolerance of the children.

www.ingramcontent.com/pod-product-compliance
Lightning Source LLC
Chambersburg PA
CBHW012042140726
47991CB00011B/3238